O   N   E   H   G

OneHourWiz™
Internet Freelancing
(Easy to Implement Ways to Make a Little or a Lot of Extra Money on the Internet)

By
Rachel Vine

**ASPATORE
BOOKS**

Published by Aspatore Books, Inc.

For information on bulk orders, sponsorship opportunities, licensing, author speaking engagements or any other questions please email store@aspatore.com. For corrections, comments or any other inquiries please email info@aspatore.com.

First Printing, November 2001
10 9 8 7 6 5 4 3 2 1

ISBN: 1-58762-003-0

Cover design by James Weinberg

Edited by Ben Lewis, Emily Dunn

Material in this book is for educational purposes only. This book is sold with the understanding that neither the author nor the publisher is engaged in rendering legal, accounting, investment, medical, or any other professional service.

This book is printed on acid free paper.

Special thanks to Adam Jaquette, Tim and Barbara Sasser, John Vine, Timothy Sasser, George and Mary Helen Brown, Leslee Jaquette, Tobias Jorda, Peter Graif, Daniel Delgado, Tim Roth, Jacque Apelian, Brett Harvey of the American Society of Journalists and Authors, Allison D. Takeshita, CPA, the endizza, the DBC, and Basil and Orbit, the copyediting cats.

OneHourWiz™

The Legendary, World-Famous Method to Mastering Anything in an Hour

How do I become a OneHourWiz?

OneHourWiz is a proven, unique method of learning that focuses on the fundamental principles of a topic, along with advice from industry experts, to master the most important aspects of anything in an hour. Although not always known by the name OneHourWiz, the principles behind this important method of learning have been practiced for decades by leading executives of the world's largest companies, top government officials, federal intelligence agencies, and some of the world's most renowned professors, teachers and visionaries.

Most people do not realize that when trying to learn a new subject or topic, they spend 80% of their time not focusing on the right principles. If they were to receive instruction from the right teachers, focused on the right principles, they could learn anything in a fraction of the time. However, getting all of these industry leaders, teachers and visionaries together would be virtually impossible. Therefore, our OneHourWiz authors collect the most important pieces of information from these individuals, pour through volumes of research, talk with industry leaders and present the material in a condensed and easy to understand format.

So, how is it possible to master anything in an hour? Each OneHourWiz uses a proprietary method that focuses on several core areas including: The 10 Most Important Principles, The History/Background Information, Focal Points/Technique, Interviews With Industry Visionaries, Quick Tips, Case Studies & Worksheets, Resources for Further Research, and a Key Words Glossary so you can "talk the talk." OneHourWiz guides have become overnight classics that remain with our readers for years and years as timeless guides they can always refer back to. So sit back, relax, and enjoy the following pages on your way to becoming a OneHourWiz!

About Aspatore Books
www.Aspatore.com

Aspatore Books has become one of the leading book publishing houses in record setting time by combining the best aspects of traditional book publishing with the new abilities enabled by the Internet and technology. Aspatore Books publishes the Inside the Minds, Bigwig Briefs, OneHourWiz and Aspatore Business Review imprints in addition to other best selling non-fiction and fiction books. Aspatore Books is focused on infusing creativity, innovation and interaction into the book publishing industry and providing a heightened experience for readers worldwide. Aspatore Books focuses on publishing traditional print books, while our two portfolio companies, Big Brand Books and Publishville.com focus on developing areas within the book publishing world. Aspatore Books is committed to providing our readers, authors, bookstores, distributors and customers with the highest quality books, book related services, and publishing execution available anywhere in the world.

Become a Part of
OneHourWiz™
*The Legendary, World Famous Method to
Mastering Anything in an Hour*

- Publish a Quick Tip on an Upcoming Topic
  (50-5,000 words)

- Submit an Idea to Write an Entire
  OneHourWiz

- Post Comments on the Topics Mentioned

- Read Expanded Excerpts

- Free Excerpts From Upcoming Guides

- Links for More Information on a Topic

www.OneHourWiz.com

Order These Other Great OneHourWiz™ Guides Today!

OneHourWiz: Making Your First Million

By Jon Pirone, ISBN: 1587621037

OneHourWiz: Making Your First Million presents ways for every individual to make their first million. Three main focal areas are covered including investing, starting your own business, and taking equity as a form of compensation. The guide is a very practical and entertaining look at ways for anyone to make their first million. The guide also includes interviews with some of the most successful business people of our time who explain how they "made their first million."

OneHourWiz: Becoming a Techie

By Mary Pyefinch, ISBN: 1587621045

OneHourWiz: Becoming a Techie is a whirlwind tour of computer technology presented in an easy to understand language and format that both technology novices and experts will find useful and entertaining. Readers will learn about computers, networks, programming, the Internet, telecommunications and wireless. After reading this guide, any individual will have the knowledge and guidance to "talk the talk" of the techies. The guide also includes interviews with leading CTOs from companies such as Motley Fool, Symantec, Verisign, Flooz.com and others who help break down the language of the techies!

OneHourWiz: Personal PR & Making a Name For Yourself

By Colleen Inches, ISBN: 1587621061

Have you ever wished you could sell yourself the way advertisers promote products? Wouldn't you love to say, "Hey world, here I am. I'm the best product in the market!" It's no coincidence the most successful people in business do it everyday, and so can you. Colleen Burns Inches shows you how to use self promotion in any career or aspect of your life. Inches, a former television news producer in New York City, gives you step by step instructions on getting attention, recognition and even media coverage for your ideas and events.

OneHourWiz: Internet Freelancing (Easy to Implement Ways to Making a Little or a Lot of Extra Money on the Internet)
By Rachel Vine, ISBN: 1587620030
OneHourWiz: Internet Freelancing contains the most up to date information on how to use the Internet to make a little, or a lot, of extra money on the Internet. The guide covers every opportunity available on the Internet including getting Paid-to-Surf the web, test new Internet products and services, freelance writing, part time consulting opportunities, affiliate programs, or simply getting paid on a monthly basis by having an extra task bar on your browser. Whether you are looking to make an extra $25 a month or an extra $2,500 a month, this guide will pay for itself many times over within the first month alone.

OneHourWiz: Internet and Technology Careers (After the Shakedown)
By April Griffin, ISBN: 1587620049
Want to take advantage of the perks Internet and technology companies have to offer? This guide will help make sure you know what to look for, ask the right questions, and get the right things put into writing so you have your upside (such as options and bonuses) and downside (guaranteed employment clauses) covered. You've heard the hype. Now learn how to use all the buzzwords with authority. Discover the workplace trends - where the hot jobs can be found, the training you need, and the salary to expect. Read interviews with recruiters from international job placement firm Kforce.com as well as computerjobs.com. Regardless of whether you are already in the Internet and technology industry or are looking to break through, this is the guide for you!

OneHourWiz: Stock Options
By Vivian Wagner, ISBN: 1587621053
Stock options are being granted to record numbers of employees, but many people receiving stock options don't really understand what they are. This guide gives you the information you need to make informed decisions about stock options, including how to value them and your company, the difference between Incentive Stock Options (ISOs) and Nonqualified Stock Options (NQSOs), the tax consequences of exercising your options, as well as information for those who want to get into options trading on their own-in an easy to understand language and format. This OneHourWiz guide also includes interviews with noted experts in the field, lawyers from some of the top law firms in the world, CFOs from companies such as Hoovers, LifeMinders,

Register.com, a sample stock option plan from Intel, and worksheets to help you keep track of your stock options.

OneHourWiz: Landing Your First Job
By Andrew Goldsmith, ISBN: 1587620253

Are you a college senior terrified to graduate? Or a freshman with a lot of foresight? This is the guide you need to make sure your first step into the real world takes you in the right direction (and to start thinking ahead to that second step!). You'll get advice from the director of Career Services at one of the hottest Ivy League schools in the country and advice from such experts as the head of recruiting from PriceWaterhouseCoopers. You'll read the stories of people who just a few years ago were standing exactly where you are, and are now establishing themselves at dotcoms, consulting firms, finance jobs, and even in the publishing, entertainment and theater scenes!

OneHourWiz: Public Speaking
By Sporty King, ISBN: 1587621096

OneHourWiz: Public Speaking can help anyone master the art of public speaking. Whether giving a presentation to a few individuals, presenting to thousands of people, or just wanting to speak more confidently to others, this guide will give you all of the keys to success as a public speaker in an easy to understand format and language. This proprietary process used to become a public speaker employed by Sporty King, a renowned public speaker, is sure to get you speaking confidently in no time.

New Titles Available Every Month!

Visit Your Local Bookseller Today!

Visit www.OneHourWiz.com for a Complete List of Titles

OneHourWiz™
Internet Freelancing
(Easy to Implement Ways to Make a Little or a Lot of Extra Money on the Internet)

Core Area 1

The 10 Most Important Principles

The following is, in essence, a cheat-sheet to the entire book in condensed, abbreviated form. It's a good reference and a good starting point for those just starting out in freelance pursuits. Even the most advanced Internet connoisseur will realize that finding a moneymaking outlet isn't easy. Job searching, which is what freelance searching is on a larger scale, is never easy. Patience, discipline, and an optimistic frame of mind will make the tedious process less frustrating and more fun.

1. Get to Know the Internet

Sit down and relax: surfing the web is going to take awhile. This step may seem a touch obvious, but it's crucial to making the most money possible. Stay away from the chat room and learn how to make the most of a search engine. Close your e-mail and look around for topics and sites that pertain to you. Bookmark these by saving the links on your browser. Writing down site links is not only time consuming, but annoying as well (and detail is key; every character is vital). Be patient; the process, as well as the job search, may take awhile.

THE 10 MOST IMPORTANT PRINCIPLES

2. Set Aside Time for Your Freelance Endeavors

Fifteen minutes here and there may land you a job, but it won't do wonders for your freelancing income, especially with Paid-to-Surf programs. Get in the habit of developing an Internet schedule and sticking to it. Save an hour every night dedicated to the Web. If a daily routine doesn't work for you, spend a couple of hours one night a week searching for freelance opportunities and pursue them throughout the week. Searching on a Monday may land you better results than searching on a Friday because job opportunities are commonly listed on the first day of the workweek. If they sit for five days, who knows how many people may have applied for the job, or whether or not someone has already been offered the position. Likewise, keep your auctioning organized by dividing your time. Save one day for listing items, another day for shipping. However, communicate constantly.

3. Develop New Moneymaking Habits

Begin Internet surfing with a search engine that pays. Find an e-mail service that pays you each time you open mail. Sign up for a Paid-to-Surf program, and enable it each time you are on the web. Give the password to family members and friends you share your computer with so they can bring money in for you, as well. Pocket change can go a long way, but on the same note…

4. Ask Yourself if it Pays Off

You're defeating the purpose of Internet freelancing if you've quit your job to spend time at home on a Paid-to-Surf program that pays $.15 an hour. Likewise, don't dedicate yourself to a lengthy project where the pay is slim unless you see it having potential to build your freelance career (or if you truly believe in the cause…it doesn't have to be all about greed, you know).

5. Be Professional

Though half the allure of freelancing is web-designing in your boxers, put your pants on when it comes to meeting clients. Treat appointments, phone calls, and correspondence with the same professionalism you would at any other job, even if the assignment is for no pay. Stay organized by creating files for assignments and setting aside a Rolodex or address book specifically for your Internet contacts. You are your own CEO, middle management, and worker ant.

6. Do Your Homework: Learn About Your Potential Employers or Clients

Do a bit of research on the site you are requesting writer's guidelines from, the Paid-to-Surf program you are thinking about signing up for, or the company you may be designing for. What kind of company are they? Do they have a reputation for paying on time? Does your style match up with theirs? Are they good

15

to their freelancers? All this information can be found on the web if you dig around.

7. Adhere to Deadlines Like Band-Aids on a Raw Wound

Nothing screams amateur like missing a deadline. Not only could missing a due date cost you the assignment; it could also cost you future assignments or references for prospective employers. If you need extra time, talk to your employer. Avoid holing up in your apartment for a week and refusing to check your e-mail. Auctioners should send items out as soon as the check clears, or face an onslaught of angry bidders via bad feedback.

8. Keep in Touch

Don't let former partners/clients/employers/bidders slip through the cracks, especially if you had a good working relationship. Drop an occasional e-mail with ideas for a project, an item they may like, or ideas on upgrading their web site. Keep notes on them in a file or notebook, including the correct spelling of names and titles, if applicable. Remember them during the holidays with a card. Communicating outside of the project insures a possible moneymaking opportunity in the future and builds trust, a necessity in any working situation.

THE 10 MOST IMPORTANT PRINCIPLES

9. Learn the Bare Minimum of (gasp!) HTML and Build a Site

Yes, it's true, and I'm sorry. In order to succeed in Internet Freelancing, it helps to know a smidgen of HTML. "Why?" you ask, "I'm a writer!" For many reasons, my program-o-phobic friend. In the age of third-graders designing web pages, many sites ask that resumes be sent via a web link, which requires you to put the blasted thing on the Internet. If you're a web designer, or are thinking about becoming one, you have no choice. It helps to learn web design before you take assignments (rather than train as you go), so that you can create a portfolio for clients to view. If you are a consultant, a site can serve as a business card where you list your skills, recommendations, past employment, and other necessary info. A web site is also great publicity: throw the link in the signature section of your outgoing e-mails. Writers can use the site to post samples of their work, which is cheaper than faxing or mailing samples individually to every prospective employer. Auctioners can list what items they are currently auctioning and where, attracting bidders. Paid-to-Surf users can have friends log into Paid-to-Surf programs through their site, collecting a referral fee from the program. If the thought of designing a web page makes you nauseous, read through the section on web design for ideas, explanation, and moral support.

10. Protect Yourself

Above all, know your rights. Know how long you have to wait for a bidder to send you a check before reselling the item. Know

THE 10 MOST IMPORTANT PRINCIPLES

how long you have before you can take action against a web site who has yet to pay you for an article, and the difference between various rights sold. Know what you can claim on your taxes. Know various legal routes you can take. You are freelancing to make money, and nothing is worst than getting ripped off or being taken advantage of. Avoid these potentially damaging situations by knowing your rights.

Core Area 2
Background Information

How often do you use the Internet? How much do you pay to use it? Do you get any money in return?

If you're like a lot of people, you use the Internet on a regular basis. Maybe you do research for school or e-mail clients. Maybe it's the way you keep in touch with loved ones far away. Or maybe you work for an online company. And perhaps, through your online usage, you've discovered little perks. Maybe you've found online discounts on plane tickets, you may have a free e-mail account, or use a free Internet service provider. Taking advantage of these services puts you ahead of the game. But what if I told you there were ways to make money on the Internet just by doing the things you do normally? Would you be willing to be paid for using search engines, checking your e-mail, and spending time online however you'd like? And what if I told you that by working an extra hour or two everyday, you could make thousands extra per year? Nowadays, it seems like everyone's making a small fortune off the Internet. Do you ever feel like it's time you cashed in, too?

In my sophomore year of college, I needed a way to make money. While browsing through my campus' job site, I came across an ad requesting a freelance technical writer for an Internet appliance site. Though I had no writing experience (and

19

my technical skills were nothing to brag about), I applied. I worked on a sample piece, they liked it, and soon I was holding a steady freelance gig that worked within my tight school/work schedule and paid $15 an hour. The site recently went under, but my experience there landed me other paying gigs. Soon, I was making enough to cover my living expenses, book fees, and weekends out (it wasn't cheap living in New York City). Talking with friends, I learned that I wasn't alone. Lots of college kids out there were making money off the Internet. It was easy. Most spent a lot of time on their computers, using them as a source of communication, a research database, or as a way to make friends (Freshman year can be a lonely one). As they took advantage of the free web access their schools offered, they were learning and understanding the way the machine and the Internet worked. Upgrading, downloading, and programming were terms that did not leave them dumbfounded, but, after time, became a way of life. The explosion of sites like Napster (www.napster.com), MP3 (www.mp3.com), and X Drive (www.xdrive.com) introduced students to file sharing and interacting in a way that expanded beyond the common "chat." They were no longer afraid of their computers, and they devised ways to make their machines work for them. Not all of these moneymaking schemes were legal or morally sound (which included selling concert bootlegs, copies of expensive programs, and homemade pornography), but they did ease the burden of a college kid's financial woes. Or, at the very least, added a little side income to Mom and Dad's monthly allowance.

People I've known have made thousands on Internet auctioning, web design, and writing. Plenty of them spend so much time on the Internet (for work or pleasure) that they sign up with companies who will pay them for every hour they are on the Internet and to look at advertisements that continually flash on their screen. Many serve as guinea pigs, signing up for and trying out new products for cash. And for some, their experience freelancing on the web directs them toward a career goal or future endeavor.

The goal of this book is to provide you with the same reassured, bold, risk-taking attitude that these students have. Ingenuity is not limited to the young. We all have the skills and abilities necessary to make the Internet work for us, despite how old or young we may be. It's just a matter of understanding what we are good at, and utilizing it to its maximum potential. Experience, time constraints, creativity, determination, and desperation may all play a role in how you earn your extra income and how much profit you take in.

This book is by no means a road map. It is physically impossible to tell you how to make money on the Internet because nothing is foolproof, and because the web is constantly evolving and changing at such a rate that nothing is certain. Rather, this book is like a compass, pointing you in the right direction. In this book, I give you jumping-off points: places to research, some general ideas. You make it work for you. Perhaps you are looking to go out on your own, without any help from anyone. Or perhaps you are looking to make friends, meet business partners, and find your own little niche within an Internet community. Whatever the circumstances may be, you'll find that this book is general enough to give an all-inclusive overview of current money making ideas on the Internet, but specific enough to allow you to tailor it to your needs.

BACKGROUND INFORMATION

Each section focuses on a different aspect of Internet Freelancing: how to get started, case studies and samples, talks with companies on their freelancing policies, and an index of sites to visit. I find the case studies and the interviews to be the most important. When it comes to e-business, the best sources of information are anecdotes rather than statistics. In such an impersonal environment, the personal touches are what make a site, or an individual for that matter, succeed or fail.

There are millions of sites on the web, and the numbers rise everyday. Domain names are growing in size to facilitate the rapid expansion of Internet companies. The immediacy of Internet business is both enticing and menacing to many companies, especially those who have yet to make their mark. Many are finding that in order to keep up with their competitors, they must have the capability to perform transactions with clients on the web. And then there's the start-up phenomenon. It's common to watch investors pour millions of dollars into an Internet startup, just to watch it flounder before it's even launched. People lose their jobs, CEOs carry a terrible burden on their shoulders as they move on to a new company, and all the energy and resources dedicated to this site is lost forever, as though it never existed. There is a lot of money to be made on the Internet from consumers willing to pay, and the most secure way to go about in making it is to work as a freelancer. You are not dependent on such an undependable income source, you have freedom and flexibility in your work, and you have no commitments, other than completing your assignment. As a freelancer, you also have a first-hand glimpse into the future of those you work for, which can be a strong determining factor should the talk of "full-time employment" ever arise.

Internet companies are looking to the people now more than ever to provide the much-needed content for their sites. Businesses are looking to independent professionals for consulting purposes. Sites are paying the public to read through e-mail and determine what is and isn't junk. The need for worker ants is high.

The Internet can be your portfolio, your business card, or your storefront. Not only can it make you money, it can save you money as well. Advertising, e-mail, and Internet space all run cheaply, if not free. And within the tangled, jumbled, overcrowded web lies a vast resource, much of which is undiscovered by the general public. Hack through the overgrowth, and it's all yours for the taking.

To get the most out of this book, you need Internet access. You need to be able to go online and utilize the resources that are there. Writing is the only activity that does not take up much computer time. It's possible to do your research in periodicals and construct your rough drafts by hand before inputting them into the computer.

If you have a computer but no Internet Service Provider (ISP), you have a few options. Services like AOL, Earthlink, Prodigy, and Compuserve are the most reliable, but usually charge a monthly fee. However, many offer free bonuses when signing up, like digital cameras or scanners, and all have special benefits available only to members. Net Zero and Blue Light are two popular ISPs that provide service free. However, count on a slow connection and ads popping up on your screen. DSL and cable connections connect to the web faster than a standard 56K, but are a bit more expensive.

Are you ready to get started? Ready to start paying back that car loan? Ready to start saving for retirement? Ready to get that new skateboard you've been drooling over? Let's begin…

Core Area 3
The Focal Points

Freelance Writing

What's the one thing all web sites need? Content (with the exception of a few: check out www.suberbad.com). Words are what bring surfers to a site and keep them there, and "wordsmiths"— those with that rare, raw talent of throwing words together into melodious harmony or those with a big thesaurus — are in high demand. Recently, web sites have been searching for writers with a punchy, sexy, quick-to-the-point and cut-to-the-chase attitude. Surfers lose interest faster than a T3 connection. What these sites want, particularly those that are retail-based, are writers who can get their point across in a quick, precise, cutting-edge manner. Enter the freelancer.

Companies like freelancers for various reasons. A freelance writer is hired for one assignment, with the possibility of more. They are paid either by the assignment or by the hour, but not by salary. Employers do not have to offer them benefits like health or dental, and they do not have sick leave or vacation time. Freelance writers come and go, and the good ones stick around for a while. But these aspects don't just benefit the bigwigs. With these traits, freelancers are given freedom and flexibility. They are not bound to one company and they are not expected to

THE FOCAL POINTS

be loyal to a certain idea or product. It is understood that freelance writers take on multiple tasks, and it is understood that many writers work from their homes as well. Freelancing can be your career or a lunchtime task.

Web writing can generally be divided into three categories: creative, informative, and technical. Creative freelance writing is not limited to the sullen, misunderstood netizen lamenting technology, pop culture, and their high school years. Many sites are searching for talented creative writers of various genres and pay on publication, though not as substantially as informative or technical writing might. Still, why not pick up $20 for that poem you thought up in the shower? Informative writing is just that: non-fictional, educated commentaries ranging from the top five SUVs to drive to the nightlife of Rio. Knowing something about your neighborhood, a politician, a foreign country, Stanley Kubrick, restoring old Chevy Novas, raising kids, or a fabulous restaurant can land you as much as a $1.00 a word. For a 1,000 word piece, that's not too shabby. Technical writing pays the most, but its tedious nature makes it difficult to do casually. Usually sought after by computer and electronic companies, technical writers are often given the task of "dumbing down" manuals or paperwork for the general populace, or asked to put into words various technological processes. This type of job requires time, patience, a dictionary, and a vague idea of what it is you are writing about, but if it's something you enjoy, by all means cash in.

Depending on how much you enjoy writing and how much time you can dedicate to the task, freelance writing is an excellent way to not only pick up cash, but also build a portfolio of your

THE FOCAL POINTS

abilities. If you're looking to earn mad money, a bit piece here or there written on a Sunday night gives you just that. If you're looking to pay off that student loan, you'll have to work a little harder. The best way to land a freelancing position is to get your work out there. Sites like well-rounded writers. Sticking to one general topic as your forte, like hiking Catalina Island or writing haikus, will limit you in the projects you are available for. Broaden your horizons. If you enjoy sports, look into writing not only about football and the World Cup, but women's basketball, international lacrosse teams, and the politics behind it all. If you like fashion, the outdoors, sex, or entertainment, cover your bases and be inclusive of everything and anything. Build your portfolio with pieces that showcase your interests and expertise (and yes, knowing the name and planet of birth of every Star Trek character counts as expertise). Think about the various topics you know a lot about, or information that is accessible to you through work (but not confidential stuff). Mix up your writing assignments, varying not only topics but genres as well. Picking up creative, informative and technical assignments of varying lengths highlights your skills and places you in demand. And should an assigned topic leave you blocked, don't be afraid to do a little research on the Web to familiarize yourself.

Where to Start

Most sites (at least those that pay decently) are looking for writers who have been published before. Why? This shows that the writer is not only credible but talented as well. Published writers carry on an air of distinction to those around them because the act of getting published seems difficult. But it's not. What constitutes a published work? A published work is simply a written piece accessible by the public. Newspapers, magazines, and books are all obvious examples, but being published on the Internet, in a school paper, or a church bulletin all counts as well.

So where does one go to get started? For you informative types, ride on over to Epinions (www.eopinions.com) and sign up. Epinions is a site dedicated to honest, truthful reviews by the public for the public. These reviews cover everything from last night's Ally McBeal to Titleist golf balls. Once you join (at no cost) and open your account, you can begin writing your own opinions on places and products. You are paid $.01 to $.03 for each time a registered member clicks on your opinion and reads it (the amount varies based on how long your review is and how much of it the member reads). Epinions pays out their Eroyalties in $10 increments. It's quick, it's easy, and you get paid continually, whether you're online or not. Best of all, you have in your hands a published work. Anyone can type in the subject on the site and find your opinion. This site is perfect for newcomers because it's very user-friendly. It also appeals to people of all ages because its topics are so varied. The trick with Epinions is to write as many reviews as you can conceive. One review may not bring in much, but five or 10 reviews can.

Creative writers can start at Rosedog (www.rosedog.com).
By signing up as a member, you are entitled to put up as many writing samples as you wish for free, with no limits and no censorship. These pieces are catalogued and prefaced by a brief description of the work (which you write) for perusal by readers,

THE FOCAL POINTS

the target audience being agents and publishers. For your convenience, the site tracks how many times people open and review your manuscript. This site also focuses on the business needs of agents and publishers, helping to expose them to the large, anonymous pool of literary talent that exists on the Internet — you (no promises here).

Technical writers need to take a different route. There are not many large databases on the Internet containing the portfolios of technical writers on display ("Joe, I found that piece you wrote explaining the process of thermonuclear fission riveting."). Tech pieces usually belong to the companies that sent out for them (see Work for Hire), and are kept either on their site or in their files. The best way to get started then is to bypass the portfolio building nonsense and get to work. Taking a class in Technical Writing (usually offered by technical temp agencies — check your phone book) often looks appealing to employers, and will give you samples to send out with your resume.

As you go along, keep in mind that you're not solely limited to these or any other options placed before you in this book. The web is constantly evolving as a speed that makes it difficult to document (Edition Two coming soon to a bookstore near you). Utilize your search engines, and try underground ones to keep the mix fresh. Dogpile (www.dogpile.com), Google (www.google.com) and Ignifuge (www.ignifuge.com) all dodge the mainstream (a.k.a. they nix the advertising) and still produce well-stocked results. As an added bonus, Ignifuge pays each time you use their search engine (for more information, see Other Ways).

THE FOCAL POINTS

Getting published is simple. If you know friends with homegrown sites, ask if you can write for them at no charge. Sure, recording Aunt Maude's 73rd birthday SOUNDS lame, but if written with a sense of humor and a lively manner, you could get a gig out of it. It's wise to have a piece on the Web that potential employers can refer to on their own. Also, consider the fact that many e-zines are constantly on the lookout for new, fresh writers, even if they are not publicizing it. Don't be afraid to e-mail sites directly and pitch ideas to them, or offer your writing services to the site. Be aggressive, be bold. You're in this for the money.

PS: Deep within the archives of Novalearn, a Web site dedicated to writer's resources (www.novalearn.com/wol/archives/fowly3a.htm) lies an article for those faced with the task of writing on something they have no clue about. Under the facade Stay at Home Travel Writing, this short, informative piece teaches you everything you need to know about faking your way through a travel piece without leaving your couch. With the help of popular resources (the newspaper, medical guides, WWW), you can write as though you've been to New Delhi and back without getting that costly yellow fever vaccination.

Now What

After you've acquired some published pieces for your blossoming portfolio, it's time to hit the big leagues and find a job. Project. Assignment. It's all the same.

THE FOCAL POINTS

Some sites offer money for your articles regardless of experience or expertise. Besides Epinions, Suite 101 (www.suite101.com) is constantly on the lookout for "Contributing Editors" for their site. Editors write a column for the site, subject matter chosen by them, either weekly, bi-weekly, or monthly. Each time a new column is up the editor gets paid. It's an excellent way to get a steady (though meager) cashflow running and build up the portfolio, all in one shot. Bookmark the site for their excellent web-related resources and freelancer tips. Write for Cash (www.writeforcash.com) also accepts informative pieces on anything. They pay per article, based on relevance and how well the piece is written, then publish the piece as its own page, promoting solely through search engines. They look for "how-to," explanatory pieces, ranging in topics from how to perform CPR to how to prune a dogwood tree.

For a freelance writing assignment, Monster, HotJobs, and other generalized job banks aren't always the best options. Usually the freelance selection is rather meager and outdated, if it exists at all. Rather, save these as a last resort and go to a site that specializes in placing freelance writers. Type "freelance writer+job" into your search engine of choice, and watch the selection grow. Some of these sites will be solely about the art of freelance writing, with plenty of articles, updates, and other miscellaneous info. These sites are somewhat helpful, but time is a-wasting. Below is a list of some of the best freelance job sources, as well as some obscure sites worthy of perusal.

www.freelancewriting.com: Sure, it seems like an obvious choice, and it is. They have the most up-to-date, well-stocked database of freelance jobs around. The site is easy to use, there are plenty of listings, and the job descriptions are longer than a sentence. You can contact employers directly from the site via an e-mail link, which saves time. Freelance Writing is a writing network, with chat rooms, articles, and information about groups and associations for writers of all inclinations. But the best job listings on the Web are found here.

www.freelancewrite.about.com: This site's array of links and valuable information on New Media writing make it a fabulous bookmark. It's packed with information of style guides, training and education, and the "other" forms of freelance writing, such as grant writing and business writing. Refer to this site for their informative articles on the "freelance scene."

www.earthweb.com: Visit for their techie-focused job database and information the computer industry.

www.writersdigest.com: This site has an EXCELLENT, highly recommended guideline database for magazines, a plus if that's your forte. They also have a thoroughly researched "Hot List" for the top 100 Magazines to freelance for. Check out the ever-so-valuable article "Write Knock-Dead Query Letters" (www.writersdigest.com/wd0201/business.html).

www.dice.com: THE site for technical writers, among other computer-oriented sorts. They have a very impressive job bank consisting of both full time and telecommute/freelancing gigs.

www.sunoasis.com: If you are somewhat computer proficient (a.k.a. you know how to check your e-mail), this site may be a bit insulting. But if you're a newcomer to the Web, this site's for you. Sunoasis dumbs down the process of freelance writing into easy to follow baby steps. They go a step further by teaching you how to use a search engine, how to doll up your resume, and other useful tips. They have prime job listings for writers divided into easy-to-follow categories: freelance, telecommute, and regionally listed full-time jobs.

Your Rights as a Writer

One of the most frustrating aspects of being a writer is worrying about whether or not you are going to get paid, a legitimate fear. It is not uncommon (and unfortunately not illegal) for sites to wait weeks, sometimes months before paying their freelancers. Writers are at the low end of the totem pole, and many aren't paid until the web site's staff and debts are paid off. But what if you don't get paid at all? What if the site goes bankrupt? Who do you turn to?

There is also the very real threat of being taken advantage of. As a general rule of thumb, you should never have to pay money in order to make money. Plenty of scams begin this way: the writer pays a reader's fee, an agent's fee, a "processing" fee, or a publishing fee to get their work on a site. More often than not, the work is never published, and the writer is out $5, $10, or $50, depending on how naïve she is. My point is this: there are plenty of ways to make money as a writer without having to pay a dime. Sites out there are looking for writers. Scout around, and do research. If the offer sounds too good to be true, it probably is.

Many writers, not-for-profit groups, and writer's associations tackle these subjects and post them on their sites for other writers to index. These sites range from personal experience to full-fledge legal counsel. As a jumping-off point, check out The Write Page's section on Writer's Rights (www.writepage.com/rights.htm). It covers plagiarism and copyrights, as well as an author's checklist for scams and schemes she may encounter along the way.

The Science Fiction and Fantasy Writers of America have a page devoted to keeping writers updated on conartists and scammers. Writers Beware (www.sfwa.org/beware) covers not only the bad guys, but also basic copyright laws and links.

The National Writers Union (www.nwu.org) also keeps an updated list of articles and recent press pertaining to writers mot being paid, companies going against their contracts, and all other evil doings that may occur. More on the NWU is found under Associations to Join.

There are certain instances where an author may need to prove that she conceived an idea first, or wrote a manuscript before someone else. ProtectRite (www.ncronline.com) is the National Creative Registry's intellectual property protection site. For a fee, they will preserve and register your manuscript within their files for 10 years, after which you must renew registration. They encrypt and secure your manuscript, and provide long-term storage accessible only to you (should your original be destroyed). They accept any written material: songs, poems, screenplays, novels, short stories, ideas, outlines, or theses. The time and day you register the item serves as the "conception" date (proof that you really did "think of it first") and can be used in court, should you ever need it. It's a good way to immediately protect your work while waiting for copyright, although it, like other protection services, should never replace copyright. Do you need to copyright your work? Read on…

What if I don't get paid?

According to Brett Harvey, Executive Director of the American Society of Journalists and Authors (and formerly a Grievance Officer with the National Writer's Union), the best way to avoid this nightmare is to sign a contract that guarantees payment. If some time passes and you still haven't received a check, talk with your editor, NOT with the accounting department. "The accounting department has no control over payment," she warns. "Wait it out, then write a letter, not an e-mail, to the editor, reiterating your demands and giving deadlines." If your editor doesn't contact you, or fails to comply, prepare to take them to small claims court. If you are the member of a writer's organization, talk with a grievance officer.

The site went bankrupt before they paid me. What can I do?

Unfortunately, very little. Harvey recommends using caution when taking on an assignment from a start-up venture. "Start with a small assignment and see how promptly you get paid. If the first assignment goes well, and you get paid on time, take another. But don't take the second before you've been paid for the first." Once Chapter 11 is filed, however, you're out-of-luck.

THE FOCAL POINTS

Writers are not "assured creditors," and rarely get paid in bankruptcy proceedings.

Once I hand over the piece I wrote, does it become their property, or do I still have some owner ship over the piece (can they publish it and sell it to whomever)?

This is a touchy subject: rights. And before you sign ANYTHING, it's a good idea to know the terminology and exactly what it is you are signing. Plenty of people, including myself, have unknowingly signed away all ownership of their piece, a devastating loss if it's a manuscript or large body of work. Keep in mind that unless you sign something, the piece is yours, and you claim all rights to it. You do not have to submit it and reprinting is not allowed. The piece is yours for you to do whatever you please with it. But most sites are not that stupid, and most writers aren't that lucky. You will, most likely, be given a contract (or e-mailed a document), and asked to read it and sign it. First off, don't let the big words and long-winded sentences scare you. Make a photocopy of the document, sit down with a pen and a highlighter, and jot notes on the page. Break down the contract, highlighting concerns and phrases you don't understand. Talk to people with some knowledge of writing, law, or contracts about the document. If need be, or if your work is huge, talk with a lawyer. Usually, for a fee, they will sit with you and break down the contract into easily digested pieces. The lawyer should be a last resort, and be used only in the most desperate of circumstances. Don't see one if she costs more than the article is worth. You also have the right to ask the employer questions about the contract. Anything you don't understand should be addressed to them. Hang on to any sort of correspondence they send you concerning the assignment or the contract. Propositions and discussions about the work can be considered binding contracts themselves, because they show what the employer wants from you and spells this out clearly. Also, keep in mind that no contract is set in stone. If parts of the document don't sound "right," "fair," or as if they work to your advantage, say something and prepare to offer another deal or negotiate before signing.

The following are common rights employers ask their writers to sell. Knowing exactly what they mean can help you make an educated choice on what to sign and why. Note that these descriptions are not just limited to the Internet. Magazines, newspapers, and periodicals all follow these guidelines as well.

FIRST SERIAL RIGHTS: When a writer signs away first serial rights, she is signing away the right for a site to publish the piece for the first time, meaning it has never been published on any site before. The prestige is that the site is getting the news, article, or story before anyone else.

SECOND SERIAL (REPRINT) RIGHTS: Second serial rights allow a site to publish your article after it's been published on a different site. The beauty of reprint rights is that they may be sold to all different sites, allowing the author to cash in more than once on a piece.

SIMULTANEOUS (ONE-TIME) RIGHTS: Simultaneous, or one-time, rights allow the site to publish the work only once. Like reprint rights, these may be sold to more than one site.

WORK FOR HIRE: These rights are commonly used and sold by freelancers. When the freelancer is hired on for an assignment, all work she develops for the employer belongs to the employer, including the copyright. Similar to All Rights (see below), the employer has all publishing and reprint rights, and may do so without notifying the author. When you sign this contract, you are giving up all rights in the piece forever. Unless there is a confidentiality clause (such as in ghostwriting), you retain authorship, but nothing else. If there is a confidentiality clause, then you may never reveal that you are the true author of the work. Writers just starting out often sign this sort of agreement, usually because they are being offered a large amount of money or because they are anxious to be hired and have a piece published. There is nothing wrong with signing this sort of agreement as long as you are aware of the consequences.

ALL RIGHTS: When you sell all rights, you keep authorship of the piece, but nothing else. The publisher can publish and reprint the piece any way she'd like without paying you. You cannot publish, redistribute, or write sequels to your piece. It is out of your hands. While Work for Hire agreements are often settled prior to writing the piece, All Rights is sold afterward the piece is developed. Proceed with caution, especially if the piece is a large manuscript, document, or body of work. Weigh the time you invested in the piece against what they're offering to pay you, and ask yourself if it's enough.

ELECTRONIC RIGHTS: Electronic Rights is a fuzzy region because the whole concept of electronic publishing is still very new, having only recently been brought into the limelight by writers suing publications. However, seeing how you're

THE FOCAL POINTS

publishing your piece online, the term will creep into the contract. Usually these rights refer to publishing the piece into electronic form, such as an e-book, online on a web site, or in a database. But ask. Make sure it's all clearly spelled out for you.

If you don't like the terms of your contract, speak up. Don't sign anything you feel uncomfortable signing, and ask questions when you don't understand something. The worst thing you can do for yourself as a writer is selling your work without knowing what you are getting out of the deal. And though not every group is out to take advantage of freelancers, an ignorant freelancer is a blessing and a godsend. Stay informed by referring to the sites listed above, or by frequenting the pages of the American Society of Journalists and Authors (www.asja.org). They highlight updated news pieces on court cases between writers and their employers, and feature the various contract-negotiating policies of major publishing houses and publications, submitted discreetly by writers.

Is there a site where I can complain about my employer, to warn future writers from suffering the same fate I have?

The best part about writing for the Internet is the community that comes along with it. "Most writer's associations," claims Harvey, "have their own chat rooms and forums for members to talk." Also, write a letter of complaint to the site's editors and, if applicable, to the parent or publishing company of the site.

Should I copyright my work? How should I do this?

Many will claim you do not need to copyright your work, because you automatically retain copyright to your work unless you specifically sign the rights away. "True, " says Harvey, but your copyright is useless unless you register. In order to claim statutory damages and legal fees (the reasons you're most likely bringing them to court in the first place), the work must be registered with the copyright office." If the piece wasn't registered, you will only be awarded actual damages, which is usually not much, if it's anything at all. Also, before you can even file your suit, you must register it. If you want the whole scoop, check out the US Copyright Office's site (http://www.loc.gov/copyright). This informative site provides detailed explanations of what copyright does and does not give you, as well as downloadable forms and an updated list of fees. It will also tell you where to send your piece, what's new in the copyright world, and what the laws are concerning international copyrights.

Copyright registration can take six months, sometimes more. But registration is effective the moment your piece reaches the Copyright office, despite the fact that the application hasn't been processed yet and that you aren't notified until the process is complete. If you want to know the date, send your item via registered or certified mail, and request a return receipt. The copyright lasts for the author's entire life, plus 70 years. After that, the copyright may be renewed by the author's estate, or the piece may become public domain. Copyright does not cover subject matter, processes or ideas, primarily because for many informative subjects, there is only one way to perform the process. Technical writers often face this challenge. The best way to work within the copyright standards is to describe the process you are discussing thoroughly and accurately, but do your own proofreading, fact-checking, and describing.

Internet Auctioning

Not since Hands Across America has our country gathered together with such force and idealistic intentions. Internet auctioning struck down in the late nineties and created a feeding frenzy for "stuff": an old Flash Gordon doll, Fire King dishware, sold-out tickets to a Bruce Springsteen concert, a million-dollar estate in Bonaire, an 'NSync member's half-eaten slice of French toast. Match this need with a booming economy and credit-card payment services, and you have the ingredients for a full-fledged open market.

The way an online auction works is simple. It's based on the "silent auction," often found at charity events and libraries. The seller places an item on display, and the buyer bids on it by writing her name and bid amount down. In this case, the seller photographs or describes the item, the buyer goes online and bids, and everyone waits. The running time of an online auction varies, but when the auction closes, usually the person with the highest bid wins. The seller and the buyer contact one another, payment and shipping addresses are exchanged, and everyone is happy…most of the time.

Online auctioning is exciting. It's accessible 24 hours a day, its selection is usually obscure and top-of-the-line, and it's suspenseful to watch, whether you're the seller or the buyer. Because the process is somewhat anonymous, with only a screen name to distinguish you from the other guy, inhibitions drop (no awkward hand raising) and bids fly. And with so many small businesses bringing their merchandise online, chances are you'll find what you're looking for.

Auction sites usually serve merely as the mediator; all transactions are between the buyer and the seller. The best sites are those that offer good customer service, such as penalties for non-payment, and a good selection. The more popular a site is, the better chance you have at selling your item for the highest price possible.

What You Need to Get Started

It's hard to delve into the world of auctioning empty-handed. First, go online, visit sites, and see what's bringing in money. Old toys in their original packaging are popular. An old place setting from a dishware company that's out-of-business sells well. When it comes to auctioning, anything is fair game. And don't just limit yourself to antiques. Elmo dolls, couture clothing, and art have all sold online and brought in hefty prices. Cars, baseball cards, and real estate sell as well. The trick is realizing and marketing the demand for what it is you have. Next, scout around for stuff to sell. Visit old thrift stores for desirables, taking care to avoid tragically hip (and brutally expensive) vintage stores or overpriced antique malls. Garage, yard, and white elephant sales, church and hospital thrift stores, pawnshops, Goodwill, and Salvation Army are all smart, practical places to look, particularly if you have a good eye.

THE FOCAL POINTS

More often than not, items that could bring in a fortune online have a sticker price of $.50. Don't be afraid to invest in a piece if you know it will bring in more in the long run. Or look around in a relative's attic, an old storage unit, or your hall closet. Think of what you have access to from work, what you have an eye for, or what you personally know a bit about. The market is vast. Chances are, you have something to sell. It's just a matter of getting it online. That old Kate Spade bag you bought last season? A souvenir quilt picked up at a roadside stand in Florida? Your mother's Barbie doll collection? Sell!

PS: If you can sell your soul, what CAN'T you sell online? Quite a few things, because most auction sites follow US Trade Guidelines. Here's a list of just some of the items banned from the auction community (a.k.a. failed attempts from desperate sellers): live animals, human body parts or remains, operating firearms, homebrews (homemade alcoholic concoctions), cigarettes, lock picking items, wild mushrooms, items made from endangered species, and items made in countries with which we have trade embargoes (think Iran, Cuba, and North Korea). Each site has its exceptions. Most auctions are lenient toward adult erotica (but stay away from "obscenity": bestiality, incest, rape, and child pornography) and antique weaponry, though with questionable items it's best to check with the site you're selling on. A complete list of eBay no-nos is found at http://pages.eBay.com/help/community/png-items.html.
Yahoo!'s blacklist is http://user.auctions.Yahoo!.com/show/tos.

Once you have your object of interest, sign up with an online auction house. EBay (www.ebay.com), Yahoo! (www.yahoo.com), and Amazon (www.amazon.com) are all popular and reliable sites that charge nothing to join. Stray from the norm, and you'll find a multitude of general interest sites. Niche sites, or specialty sites, are increasing in popularity as well, and helpful when looking for that certain oddity or rarity.

A digital camera helps when selling a one-of-a-kind piece. Many potential customers surf on by if there's no picture for them to refer to. If you don't have one of your own, try to find an image of it in a photo bank online. Or, refer to an online auction for an inexpensive camera. Look into "special offers" and "last chance deals" that ISPs are always promoting. Often they pitch in a low-quality (but hey, it works) digital camera to lure you their way. Another way to get your image online is to photograph it with a standard camera and scan the photograph onto a disk. You can then place the image onto the site. If you don't have a scanner, many copy centers have them available for use for a small fee. Bring your own disk.

Because photographs take up so much space, many sites require that you have a place online to store your images, which can be called up automatically by the auction site when someone clicks on your item. Free web sites aren't hard to acquire; most ISPs give them away to their customers. Sites like Angelfire (www.angelfire.lycos.com) and Terrashare (www.terrashare.com) also provide free web space. A picture per web page ensures the auction site will call up the correct image (you provide the link to the page when registering your item for sale). If creating a web site seems difficult, time-consuming, or just plain scary, go to Photopoint (www.photopoint.com). Photopoint allows you to store your images on their site for free. They do all the dirty work, placing

44

your images into your own "album." It's also a great site to use if you share photographs with friends and family on the Internet. Also, many of your web-based e-mail accounts (like Hotmail) give image space to their members called a "Photo Album" (or the like), which will work for auctions as well.

An item, an image, and an auction-house alias are the bare necessities of auctioning. With these in hand, there's nothing left to do but start selling.

Terminology

There are key universal terms used in the online auctioning world. Knowing what they mean could be the difference in whether your item brings in $1.00 or $100.

ENGLISH AUCTION: This is the most common type of auction. Virtually every site works according to the English auction method, unless otherwise stated. In an English auction, buyers bid the highest price they are willing to pay. When the auction is complete, the item is sold to the highest bidder.

VICKREY AUCTION: Like an English auction, buyers bid the highest price they are willing to pay for an item. However, when the auction is complete, the highest bidder wins the item at the price offered by the second highest bidder. For example, Man A bids $12 on an old platter from the 50's. Woman B bids $20, and the auction closes. The winner is Woman A, but she wins the platter for the $12 price. This type of auction is not as common but a great incentive to encourage people to bid on your goods.

THE FOCAL POINTS

DUTCH AUCTION: Dutch auctions are used in cases where the seller has more than one of a particular item to sell. Say you have 3 identical Dukes of Hazzard watches you'd like to sell starting at $5. You state your minimum bid ($5) and how many of the items you have (3), and wait for buyers to bid. The winners are those who bid the most for the items successively. If five people bid $10, $7, $6, $5, $5, the winners are the three highest bidders. The person who bids the most in a Dutch auction (here the $10 bidder) is guaranteed an item; others follow based on how much they bid. However, the price that everyone pays is the lowest successful (meaning winning) bid (here, the price all three will pay is $6). If all or a few of the buyers bid the same amount, the winners are then based on who bid first.

YANKEE AUCTION: Like a Dutch auction, buyers are bidding on multiple items. However, the winners pay what they bid (the three above will pay $10, $7, and $6 respectively), and not the lowest successful bid price.

RESERVE (i.e. a reserve bid, a reserve price, setting a reserve, etc): Set by the seller and undisclosed to the buyers, a reserve bid is the lowest amount the seller is willing to sell the item for. For example, if you have a Mickey mantle baseball card worth $200, you may place the reserve at $200 (or whatever amount you'd like to insure that you receive from it before parting with it), but begin the bidding at $10, to encourage wary buyers. Buyers are told only when they have met the reserve, not what the reserve amount is, which encourages them to keep bidding in the hopes of reaching the reserve. If the auction ends and the highest bid is lower than the reserve price set, the seller has the right not to sell the item, no matter how many bids were placed on it. If Man X only bid $55 on the card and the auction ends, Mickey stays put.

PROXY BID: Most sites have the software and the capability to provide a proxy bid service to their buyers. When bidding on an item, the buyer enters in the maximum price she is willing to pay. The computer then advances the bidding for the buyer when a person bids more than the current bid but less than the proxy bid, keeping her on top of the auction.

DYNAMIC BID TIME: You can set a dynamic bid time when placing your item up for auction. The last few minutes of the auction, as designated by you, are set into "dynamic bid time" mode, and if a buyer bids within that time frame, the auction is extended for another few minutes.

RATING: There is a brutal loyalty to accuracy and truth within the online community. Many auction sites offer a "rating system," which allows sellers and buyers to grade each other on the business deal. These ratings are then accessible by others interested in participating in a business deal with you. The ratings system may seem like a waste of time, but you'd be surprised just how seriously people take it. If you botch a deal, chances are your partner will let the public know how you messed up, and if you'll strike again. Bad ratings usually can be revoked, after the auction house comes in and mediates.

MINIMUM BID/MAXIMUM BID: A minimum bid is just that: the least amount you are willing to sell an item for, or the least amount you are willing to pay for an item. A maximum bid is the highest amount you are willing to sell an item for, or the highest amount you are willing to pay for an item.

REVERSE AUCTIONS: Reverse auctions allow people to bid on goods and services for the lowest possible price. The buyer puts an ad up, listing the maximum bid she will pay for an item, and the sellers duel it out to provide her with the lowest price.

ESCROW: Escrow is an option offered by few sites, and is usually handled by a partner of the auction site. When an auction ends, the buyer sends payment to the escrow company, and the seller ships the item to the buyer. If and when the buyer approves the item sold to her, the seller receives payment. This is a good process for those making large-scale transactions, or those afraid of getting cheated. However, both parties must agree to the service, and there is a fee, which is pinned on the buyer.

Fees

Unfortunately, most sites charge sellers various fees for utilizing the site, which usually cover the costs of running the site, paying the staff, and other miscellaneous expenses. Shop around and see which auction site is the best for you. eBay charges minimal fees that could add up, especially if your items are not worth much. But since eBay is the most popular Internet auctioning site currently running, it may pay off to sell your item on a site with so many visitors. Yahoo! Auctions, once free to one and all, now charge a selling price similar to eBay. But because Yahoo! is much smaller, fewer people visit the site, which could stifle the final selling price. Shipping and handling for an item is usually calculated by the seller (you) and paid by the buyer. If you really want your item to look appealing, include shipping and handling in the minimum bid price.

Some common fees are:

SELLING FEE: Some sites will only charge their sellers a one-time fee. Others will charge a fee based on the value of the piece after the auction. This fee is usually a small percent, 1-2.5%. There are also the sites that will charge you an insertion fee (placing the item up) and a final value fee (a percentage fee based on the item's worth after it sells).

RESERVE FEE: Some sites will charge you a small, one-time fee for setting a reserve auction. It can be either a flat rate, or a percentage of the reserve price you set.

FEATURED ITEM FEE: Some auctions allow you to bump your item from bottom of the heap to the top of the list, for a fee. These are listed before all other listings under a separate heading ("Featured Auctions," "Hot Items," etc.). Other sites will promote your items on their home page, accessing buyers before they reach the auctions. These fees will either be one-time or percentage fees. While the sites do publicize your piece, people will find you if you have a great item, so these "Featured Item" settings are often unnecessary.

Getting Paid

As a seller, you decide how you are paid for your items. Because sending cash through the mail isn't recommended, money orders are a popular way to buy items for both parties. The seller knows payment is guaranteed, and the buyer does not have to disclose any personal financial information to the seller. Money orders are cheap, and available at banks, some stores, and the post office.

Many sellers take checks. It's a convenient way for buyers to pay quickly, without having to wait in line for a money order. However, seller beware: while it is usually safe to receive checks as payments from buyers, it's a good idea to wait for the check to clear before sending out the item, avoiding a potential rip-off.

Within such a consumer-based activity, it was only a matter of time before the words "paper or plastic" came into play. With the introduction of Paypal and Billpoint, credit card acceptance was no longer limited to the store owner selling wares on auctions. Now anyone can receive payment, at no fee.

Sign up for Paypal (www.x.com), and $5 is automatically deposited in your account. Best of all, you only need an e-mail address to open your account. Before you begin selling, sign up with the site for free. Note within your item description that you accept Paypal. At the auction's conclusion, go to the site and enter the buyer's e-mail address and the amount owed to you. Paypal will hunt him down. The buyer then go to the site, enter his credit card number, and designate the amount that goes to you. Paypal then sends you a check. It's fast, it's free, and it couldn't be easier. Its use isn't limited to Internet auctioning, either. You can pay anyone with an e-mail address by credit card, and they will receive the money in check form. Your

THE FOCAL POINTS

account is also insured up to $100,000. That ought to help you sleep at night.

Billpoint (www.billpoint.com) is a service endorsed by eBay that works on a similar level. It allows credit card transactions between buyers and sellers to take place. At the end of the auction, the buyer automatically receives an invoice (constructed by Billpoint, saving you time) and pays from the link. Small transaction fees, based on whether you are an individual or a merchant seller, are charged by the company.

Tips for Selling

If you have an object that's worth quite a bit, put a reserve price on it to insure you receive what it's worth. If it doesn't sell the first time around, keep in mind that the online auction community comes and goes, and each day brings in new potential buyers.

In your one-line title of your item, be as descriptive as possible. Buyers are brought to your item based on the search words they type in. Listing what the product is, what category it falls under, and the manufacturer are all ways to reel 'em in. And go heavy on the adjectives. Don't say "old," say "vintage mod retro Sputnik lamp" or "vintage antique retro 50s Fire King Jadite Restaurantware plate." It's a mouthful, but every word has the potential to bring someone there. Also, adding incentives into your title like "no reserve" or "like new" may coax a viewer to take a peek.

Don't become discouraged if no one bids on your item its first few days online. Items are usually placed in chronological order based on how much time is left in the auction. Some sites, for an extra fee, will place your listing at the top of the heap. If you are anxious to sell, this may not be a bad idea.

It is wise to exclude shipping and handling from your auction price. After packing and wrapping, the postage due may be more than you expected, and it's not uncommon for an object to cost in postage what it did to purchase. Set the postage rate as an extra fee, and let the buyer know it's not included. To get an estimate of what the postage fee will be, go to the US Postal Service Site (www.usps.gov), click on Calculate Rates, and fill in the necessary information (zip codes of sender and recipient and weight). The prices will be listed for you, based on how quickly you want it to get there.

If you are selling something of worth or something breakable, buy insurance for it through the post office. The standard rate is around $1.80 for every $100.

In your online description, list the flaws the piece has (and be honest), but downplay them. If a plate has some scratches for constant use, note that the piece has "minor wear." Mention the chips, snags, and tears, or you could end up with angry customers. Angry customers equal angry ratings, and if you think no one reads those, guess again.

Don't send out anything until payment has been received. The moment the check clears, send the item on its way. People become rather insecure when sending their money to anonymous

THE FOCAL POINTS

faces and sometimes chicken out. Likewise, you should wait until the check clears before sending items out, to avoid a potential rip-off.

Don't be afraid to take up complaints with your auction house, unless they state that they do not get involved in disputes. Most are there to serve as a liaison between the buyer and the seller. If your buyer's not holding up to his share of the contract, turn him in. You are, after all, doing this to make money.

Leave a rating for your buyer. If they take forever to send a payment in, say so. If they were a pleasure to work with, say so. It is often comforting for people to get a bit of background history on the person they plan to do business with beforehand. Also, many people enjoy getting feedback. It's a quick and easy way to make yourself look like a good business man.

Keep in mind that the online market is inflated when compared to thrift stores and other markets. You pay for the convenience of finding the item in a nanosecond rather than hunting down every antique mall within a 50-mile radius. And when the market consists of many young professionals and teenagers from urban communities, prices are likely to soar. Set your minimum bid based on this fact. Tempt them with a low minimum, knowing full well that your item (if it's hot) will sell for much more. You're most likely to get customers when you set your rate not necessarily at what everyone else has, but rather a bit lower. Then watch the bidding war. If someone online wants what you have to offer, chances are they'll do what they must to have it.

Consulting

Within this anonymous Internet community that has taken shape over the years are people who make their living doing what it is they love to do. They stay at home, work from the Web, and still manage to write their screenplays, take the kids to soccer, or tend to their gardens. Consulting provides flexibility (you set the hours), a fun environment (what's more fun than your own house?), and no dress code for working professionals.

I Don't Get It

Tarot card readers, wedding planners, landscape designers...Consultants are people who take their skills, their loves, or their passions, and develop them into a source of income. They assume an authoritative position on the topic, and market their abilities for use by the general public. They can be people who are tired of working for someone else, people who, due to disability or illness, must stay at home, or people developing a side career from something they are good at or know quite a bit about. And often without realizing it, we all do a bit of consulting ourselves, at no charge. Helping a relative move, giving relationship advice, or going with a friend to pick out the right cordless drill are all examples of the consulting we do on a daily basis. We all know a lot more than we think we do. It's time to put that knowledge to work.

Now I Get It, But How do I Start?

Once you make the decision to go solo, the vast frontier that lies before you seems, well, mighty vast. Where to go? Where to start? What to do?

Step One: Make Decisions

First and foremost, decide who you are, what your goals are, and what your shiny new title is. Are you Tim Sasser, Independent Tax Consultant, or M. H. Brown, Medieval Historian? Are you looking to expand your project into a full-fledged home business within the year, or keep it intimate? This decision will affect the way you operate. Next, get yourself into office mode. Assign one area of your home as your office, be it a spare room, a small corner, or the kitchen table. Take over shelf space and a drawer or two. Designate hours for work, and stick to your schedule. Stay seated, and do not allow outside influences to invade your work frame of mind. Create an e-mail address for your new endeavor, and use the Signature file to promote your services on each piece of mail you send. Get business cards and letterhead made (cheap ones to start; you don't want a deficit your first day into business), or make them yourself on your computer. As boss, your business will rise or sink depending on you. Create the most efficient work area possible to get the job done.

Step Two: Study Up

Read up about your industry. A trip to the library or bookstore will uncover a wealth of how-to manuals, videos, and articles. Learn different aspects of your field. If you're going to be a

Freelance Web Designer, build upon your existing HTML skills by learning Flash. If you're an Appraiser of Victorian Furniture, read about Queen Victoria and her state policies. Many local community colleges and city centers offer various classes and forums for a small fee. Consider taking classes that compliment your new career. Stay up-to-date on your certification and licenses. Look to special interest magazines and Web sites that cover your interests. Stay informed and stay educated on the subject. As an "expert," you owe it to yourself and your clients to be in the know.

Step Three: Network

Clear your throat and warm up those typing fingers: it's time to make a name for yourself. Fortunately, the suit can stay in the closet…for now. Telephone calls and e-mail will suffice. To fill that makeshift Rolodex, get on the Web and investigate. Type your field into a search engine and see what pops up. Often, you'll come across the sites of individuals who are successful as an Indie Pro. E-mail them and ask them for tips. Also, look to the people you know. Friends of friends of family can often give the best first-hand advice. Introduce yourself and your abilities. Visiting chat rooms on sites like Bizy Moms (see below) will link you to dozens of people who are in the same boat. Make some allies. Many sites offer various services to users, including posting their resume and profile for interested parties to read. Take advantage of these free marketing ploys.

PS: Beware of people trying to sell you marketing strategies or "tips." They are consultants themselves, and may charge you hundreds of dollars for information you could have found for free. Rather, utilize that search engine and type in "work at home," "make money," or "consulting." The best help found here is often anecdotes and true stories from people who started out like you and I: without a clue on what to do next. Also, watch out for conartists looking to prey on money-desperate souls. There are plenty of work-at-home scams who seem legit on paper, but whose words deliberately deceive. At Real Jobs Online (www.realjobsonline.com/scamalert.htm), *the latest scams are revealed and broken down paragraph by paragraphs to teach others how to spot a fraud. Some warning signs of possible scams include a high front-end cost ("Buy your Vita-Happy-Life Kit to sell for $300 and make quadruple your money back!") and an ad full of* CAPITAL LETTERS AND EXCLAMATION POINTS!!!!!

Consulting Hot Spots

The following are must-have bookmarks for anyone looking to make it solo on the Net.

The premiere Web site for independent professionals both on and off line, Guru (www.guru.com) offers sage advice, fabulous job opportunities, and a site that's easy to navigate. At Guru, you can leave a profile for hirers to review, avoiding altogether the dreaded cover letter. On the other hand, their job bank is loaded and up-to-date, with great telecommute and in-house positions all over the States. Their articles cover the vitals, like publicity, taxes, and incorporating, without getting too wordy or technical. It's a nice little spot to call home, or to set as your default.

EXP (www.exp.com) puts experts within accessible reach to the general public through a number of ways. Qualified professionals (that's you) sign up at the site, filling out an expert profile that lists their qualifications, a breakdown of their background, their fees, and their schedule. From there, clients skim through the selection, searching for the professional who will fit their needs. The two connect by three ways. Call Now enables the client to reach the professional over the telephone (dialed by EXP to insure privacy). EXP keeps track of the length of the call and bills the client via his credit card. Chat Now allows the professional and the client to chat in real time online. Once again, EXP keeps track of the length of the chat and bills the client's credit card. E-mail Now allows the client to write to the professional, and is charged a flat fee for the response. You may also answer questions listed in the Public Questions Area, and charge the client. Though EXP takes a percentage of your earnings, it's a great way to advertise and be in touch with a variety of people from all over the country.

Keen (www.keen.com) prides itself on connecting people with questions to people with answers. As a consultant, you write up a profile on yourself, and what your specialties are. You create a schedule listing your availability to take calls and your "rate." This rate can be per minute, a flat fee, or per recording. Your listing is placed in a database, and when someone searches under your topic, they find your listing. There are three ways you can interact with customers. Keen can connect you over the telephone during the hours specified in your schedule, they can listen to your recorded message, or you can respond through e-mail. Your payments are placed in an account, and clients leave you a rating. The only real downfall to Keen is that it charges a connection fee, usually a percent amount they take from each charge. However, it's a great way to reach a lot of potential clients effortlessly. Though much of Keen is done over the telephone, you do not need another phone line or fancy-pants DSL in order to play. Before putting the caller through, Keen gives you 15 seconds to disconnect from your computer and await your customer. This is great for consultants of various inclinations, but those who specialize in advice or handy household tips may find themselves at a higher demand.

It's brains for the buck at Knexa (www.knexa.com), which stands for KNowledge EXchange Auction. You upload your "knowledge" (term papers, theses, manuscripts, business plans, etc.) onto the Knexa site, and bidders duke it out. What makes Knexa great is that your pieces can be sold more than once, and Knexa will, according to your preset limits, automatically adjust the price higher or lower, depending on how well the piece sells. As one in the know, you may also answer questions posted on the Knexa site, and charge for the information. You never have to worry about non-payment, because bidders must give a valid credit card number when they first register with the site. Most of the listings lean toward the business side of the spectrum, but all topics are welcomed and encouraged. Knexa also has branches specializing in sales in Europe and Australia.

One of the best resources on the Internet pertaining to consulting is Bizy Moms (www.bizymoms.com). Inspired by but not solely limited to stay-at-home-moms, Bizy Moms features articles, inspirational true-life stories ("I'm a mother of four-month-old sextuplets, and I make $2 million a year…"), ideas for those considering a stay-at-home-career but coming up short, and

THE FOCAL POINTS

business opportunities which allow you to work from home while employed by another company. While they tend to lean more toward the home business end of things rather than actual consulting, the site still provides a wealth of knowledge that's easy to use. Liz Folger, creator of the site, offers her own services as a home business consultant for a fee (a bit ironic, no?), but perusing the site may be enough.

At Ants (www.ants.com), employers list their job openings and what the project entails, and indie pros bid on it. What you bid is your expertise, your experience, and, unfortunately, what you are willing to be paid upon completion. The employers then take all the bids and filter them out, until they find the one who will get the job done. Ants will charge the consultants (that's you) a percentage fee once the job arrangement is settled. They advise that you include this fee in with your offer (if you charge $200 for a 400-word piece, charge over that to insure you make $200).

PS: Sick of registering for a site just to look around? Don't have time for passwords, codes, logins and the likes? Visit these two sites with ease:

Freelance BBS (www.freelancebbs.com) is a no-nonsense, cut-to-the-chase job site that eliminates the headhunter and connects companies with workers. Choose the profession, select Available Projects, and click Show Me The Ads. That's it. You can register and use their free site posting (a.k.a. free publicity!) and discussion boards, but for ads in a hurry, you can't beat them.

T-Jobs (www.tjobs.com) features a wide variety of telecommuting jobs without the hassle. Just choose your area of interest, and you'll be connected to related job listings. Each listing has the contact's name and e-mail and a synopsis about the position. If it was any easier to use, it'd be insulting.

Where The Money Is

What are the hottest consulting positions around? If you're any good at the following, you've got your work cut out for you...

FREELANCE WEB DESIGN: If you've a knack for Flash and HTML (or fake it by visiting www.davesite.com.webstation.html/), you'll have no trouble finding work. Many businesses looking to hop on the Internet bandwagon merely want a site up that describes who they are and their mission statement, rather than an interactive site that needs constant attention. For this job, they go to freelancers, and they pay well.

CPA/TAX ADVISOR: For taxes, for accounting, for friendship...a certified public accountant can wear many hats for businesses in need of some serious number-crunching. Be prepared to be swamped January 1 through April 15.

MANAGEMENT: The manager is the one who nurses the young, fledging actor/singer/writer/performer. She usually arranges screen tests, auditions, headshots, and interviews with agents. There is plenty of opportunities to be had as an aspiring manager, but quite a bit of leg work as well. Making contacts, schmoozing, and "asking for favors" are harder than they look. And they look so easy on TV.

CAREER ADVISOR: Think of yourself as the self-sufficient embodiment of a large staffing agency. That's career advising in a nutshell. You meet up and agree to assist a client, you send out her resume, and you make contacts with Human Resource executives at various companies. The approach you take distinguishes yourself from the rest. Do you base match-ups on similar values between the company and the client, or on the client's career goals and experience? Do you bring personality tests into the picture, matching up the client with the various fields that fit her description, or do you go with company stability and employee promotions?

"Free Money" Campaigns

Paid-to-Surf Programs

As far as advertising execs are concerned, there are no advertising boundaries. The impending threat of golden arches invading the surface of the moon is an ever-constant reminder that we live in a consumer-driven society. By those standards, Paid-to-Surf is a brilliant idea, benefiting both the advertiser and the patron. Unlike TV commercials or magazine ads, advertisers on a Paid-to-Surf program have the undivided attention of the surfer. The surfer, totally engrossed in the Internet, cannot help but look at the small box cluttering her screen. And no matter how hard she tries, she cannot block the commercials played on her Internet radio from entering her subconscious as she scrolls around. But the bonus for the surfer is that rather than be surrounded by advertisements everywhere (on the street, in stores, on TV) for free, she's getting paid, and has the choice to turn those ads off. She checks her e-mail, sells her stock, and researches a new site, all while getting paid for it.

That is the theory and practice of Paid-to-Surf programs. Surfers download software onto their computers (though some work solely through browsers) that allows the company to keep track of how long they stay on line and how actively they "surf": look around, click on ads, etc. Meanwhile, a box ranging in size from an eighth of the screen to a fourth continually flashes ads. Some companies make you click on the ads to get paid. Others don't. The surfer is paid per hour, or fraction there of, spent online. These hourly rate can vary from $.60 to $.12, depending on how popular the company is and if there is a monthly hour maximum or unlimited hours.

Recently, the problems have escalated, primarily as the drainage in funds rises. Tim is a 16-year-old sophomore in high school always on the lookout for ways to earn extra money. So when he heard about Paid-to-Surf programs from some friends at school, he signed up. The first he joined was All Advantage (www.alladvantage.com), who made his mother sign a waiver before he could join, but then the list grew. "I joined 13 different programs because it was easy. There aren't any limits to how many you can join, and I could run all of mine at the same time." Tim began accumulating hours at an abnormal rate. How? "I have DSL, so I never have to worry about tying up the phone line. I also downloaded some illegal software that moves my mouse continually, which I set up before I go to bed." Could that have anything to do with why he has never been paid? "I don't know. But it's been two months, and All Advantage still owes me for my 25 hours. So does Cash Fiesta (www.cashfiesta.com), Desktop Dollars (www.desktopdollars.com), and all the rest." Has Tim ever been paid? "No. I know a bunch of people who have, though. My best friend was recently paid $400 from All Advantage, but he didn't cheat." Tim's Paid-to-Surf endeavors were a short-live stint, lasting only about a month. "I stopped doing them. Not getting paid was beginning to frustrate me. Clicking on ads I was interested in, only to be taken to a bigger banner site frustrated me. Ads popping up before I was even logged in frustrated me most of all," he responds. While Tim's opinions don't reflect every Paid-to-Surf participant, he's not alone in his frustrations. Sites like Epinions feature the rants of surfers angry over payment (or lack thereof). But what can the programs do? These programs claim that people like Tim, people taking advantage of the system, are the reason they cannot pay their customers in the first place.

Most, if not all, Paid-to-Surf programs utilize a referral system. Think of the system as a family tree. When you spread the word about a program to a friend and they sign up, they list you as a referral. You then receive money for each time they surf. You also receive money for each time one of their referrals surf, and the list goes on. Referral programs are the way any big money is made on these programs, so it is important to spread the word.

With so many sites going up and falling down, it's difficult to write a recommendation. The following sites, however, are great sources for information, opinions, and advice:

THE FOCAL POINTS

Get Paid-to-Surf the Web (www.wolfden.linkopp.net/surf.html) is an independent guide to the latest Paid-to-Surf programs and their pay rate. They also provide links to each program.

Get Paid to be Online (www.getpaidtobeonline.net) provides information and links about not only surfing programs, but various other programs out there designed to make you money, like e-mail services, shopping, and interacting with others. Bookmark it and refer to it anytime the pocketbook's feeling a bit too light.

Pocketfiller (www.pocketfiller.com) has up-to-date news on up-and-coming programs and sites that are "dead." They also provide referral services and lists of paid-to-surf programs who pay (good to know when signing up).

Other Ways

There are many sites that don't fall into the specified categories outlined in this book. This special little spot is designated for all those "other" ways to make money off the Internet, like running screensavers (www.onscreen.com), joining an online community (www.instantagora.com), chatting (www.chat4cash.com), and downloading large files during your computer's idle time for companies (www.processtree.com). Because these sites can be volatile, look up sites like Free Money Review and Get Paid to be Online for the most recent information.

THE FOCAL POINTS

IWON (www.iwon.com): IWON is a contest, and its rules are very simple. You begin by registering with this search engine/personal companion/e-mail site. Each time you login to the site, you earn points for everything you click on, be it a search, e-mail, news headlines, or any other service they provide. These points turn into entries for a weekly, monthly, or yearly raffle for cash. While the odds seem to be considerably low, why not try to earn money for stuff you're going to do anyway?

Netflip (www.netflip.com) is a site steeped in advertising. Once you register and log in, you have the option to sign up with other sites. You can test sites, fill out surveys, or register with them to receive information on a continual basis. Every time you sign up with one of these other sites, Netflip will pay you a small amount. They keep a running total of how much you've earned, and once you hit $20, you are sent a check. A helpful hint: Unless you really ARE interested in signing up for a multitude of e-zines and the information they send you, sign up for a free e-mail account somewhere and use that address. Otherwise you'll lose yourself in the junk mail. Be sure to check that new e-mail address, however. Most of these sites require that you verify your e-mail address before they give Netflip the green light to pay you. The ad sites vary day to day, and you have to wait three days before clicking on the same site again. But it's a great way to pass the time at work or put off writing a paper, and somewhat justifiable, because you are getting paid.

By signing up with the affiliate program Linkshare (www.linkshare.com), you allow ads for various retail outlets to flash on your site. Each time one of your surfers click on these ads and makes a purchase, you receive a commission. With

THE FOCAL POINTS

some ads, a mere visit to the site earns you a bit of money. If you receive a lot of traffic on your site, this is a great way to earn money on the side.

Ignifuge (www.ignifuge.com) is a web site that pays you to use their search engine. After downloading their free software, each time you use their site, you get money. They also have a referral program that has no number limit, allowing you to earn money many levels down the line.

With Terrashare (www.terrashare.com), you are given free web space, and can earn money each time a guest clicks on a banner ad that flashes on your site. The money comes from the advertisers, with Terrashare literally sharing the wealth with its users.

RadioFreeCash (www.radiofreecash.com), the first of its kind, pays its customers to listen to the radio as they use their computers. You do not have to be surfing, you can simply be using your computer. They have hundreds of channels, over 200 genres of music, and make sure you are listening by prompting you to click a button a few times an hour.

PS: Beware Single Surfers: Expected to hit the web are Internet date services, which pay you to use chat rooms, respond to ads, and yes, go on a date. You would get money off of your lonely friends who sign up, along with the money you make using their services. While few people admit to meeting their significant others online, will anyone actually admit to getting paid while meeting their significant others online?

Core Area 4

Uncle Sam's Evil Ways: The Interview with Allison D. Takeshita, CPA

Frequently Asked Questions About Auctioning

Do I have to charge sales tax?

Allison D. Takeshita, a CPA in Honolulu, Hawaii, says that while you may not be required to charge sales tax, you may have to pay sales taxes to your state. "If you auction items on an occasional or infrequent basis, your sales can be considered casual sales, for which sales taxes are not applicable. However, if auctioning is your business, or one means of your business, then you could elect to charge sales tax because you might owe money to your state." She notes that these auction earnings are considered a part of gross income for state sales tax purposes, but that most states allow you to claim an exemption for out-of-state sales. "As a seller, you could choose to pass the sales tax on to those customers residing within your state, which, in traditional retailing, is common because it helps you fulfill your state sales tax obligations. But customers may not appreciate it because it's not general practice in the auction arena." Takeshita also points out that "the advent of e-commerce has raised some significant tax issues, and Congress has attempted to address those issues through its Internet Tax Freedom Act of 1998 and its formation of the Advisory Commission on Electronic Commerce. While legislation is still in progress, there is currently a moratorium on any new or discriminatory taxes on Internet sales in order to encourage the growth and development of e-commerce. Basically, the Advisory Commission has recommended a collaboration between state and local governments and the private sector to come up with a Uniform Sales and Use Tax Act which will lay down the same e-commerce sales tax rules for all taxing jurisdictions throughout the nation." In other words, Uncle Sam is scheming up a way to get your money, it just may take a little time.

Do I need to claim my auction earnings in my taxes?

Technically, according to Takeshita, if your auctioning activities are carried on regularly and for-profit and qualify as a business, yes. "Generally, the IRS wants you to report anything and everything. You would need to file a Schedule C, which covers business income and expenses. On the other hand, you would be able to deduct costs on this same Schedule, like Internet connection and purchases." While most individuals get away with not claiming their auction earnings, Takeshita frowns upon businesses attempting a similar game. "With businesses selling on the Web," she claims, "the income tax laws definitely apply."

Indie Pro Tax Questions

Once you start going indie pro, the finite tax lines begin to blur. Suddenly, you find yourself clinging to your familiar 1040 like a life raft in the stormy sea. Schedules? Expenses? Deductions? Yikes! Allison D. Takeshita, an independent CPA in Honolulu, comes to the rescue.

How should an independent professional go about in filing? What forms are necessary?

"The self-employed freelancer," advises Takeshita, "needs to file three forms: the standard 1040, the Schedule SE, and the Schedule C." The Schedule SE calculates how much self-employment tax you owe the government, roughly 15.3% of your earnings (making up for Medicare and Social Security costs usually provided by an employer and deducted from your paycheck). The Schedule C calculates your business income and expenses.

What counts as business expenses?

Insurance, membership to trade organizations, classes and education, travel, meals, entertainment, internet connection, office supplies...the list goes on. States Takeshita: "Basically anything reasonably pertaining to your business can be claimed as an expense and can be deducted, bringing down your net business income which is then taxed. For big items, like a car or a computer, you would usually depreciate the cost, spreading it out over a period of time--typically five years. The purpose of depreciating these items is to match your deductions against the related income it is generating."

Is there a certain amount where if you earn below that, you don't have to file?

Takeshita laughs at this one. "You always have to file. But if you make under $400 net income (like the money earned from a freelance assignment), you don't have to pay any self-employment taxes on it."

What if the indie pro has an assistant?

"In my opinion," begins Takeshita, "the best way to treat an assistant is as an 'independent contractor', which you'd note as an expense on your Schedule C. The assistant would then have to file a Schedule SE of her own and pay for her Social Security and Medicare. Otherwise, if she is treated as an 'employee', you are roped into paying those payroll taxes, which all add up."

What are the benefits of going Inc. vs not?

"Going Inc. is usually not better tax-wise because of double taxation: you are taxed at both the individual level and the corporate level," Takeshita says. "People often incorporate for non-tax reasons, the primary one being to protect their own assets. If the person as Inc. is sued, the plaintiff is limited to winning only the corporate assets. But if the person is not Inc. and is sued for work she did, the plaintiff may go after personal assets, including her house, her bank accounts, etcetera." A good middle-ground, according to the CPA, is an S-corp, which is taxed like a partnership (at the individual level only, no corporate taxes necessary), but has limited liability in a lawsuit like corporation. However, because small businesses must

71

qualify for this standing, and since each individual situation differs, Takeshita recommends that you consult your legal or tax advisor before making any changes to your form of organization.

THE FOCAL POINTS

Core Area 5

Resources for Further Research

Resources

Inkspot (www.inkspot.com) is chock-full of articles and links. Though the classified section is weak, their writer-oriented search engine is something to brag about.

101 Writing Answers and 101 Publishing Answers (located respectively at www.101writinganswers.com and www.101publishinganswers.com) have so many links to so many useful, practical writing sites that it's considered the Oracle at Delphi of freelancing sites. Classes, markets, resources, clubs…it's all here. Bookmark these sites.

Writers Write (www.writerswrite.com) is a great source for information on books, publishing, and writing. They have author interviews, writing news, a job search, and much more. Don't hold it against them that they recommend selections from Oprah's Book Club.

Associations to Join

Once you begin to make a living out of your freelance endeavors, you may want to consider joining a professional group. These groups work under two missions: to serve as an agency, or to serve as a union. They offer contract services, help with court-related issues, and fight for freelancers collectively to insure better pay.

Many freelancers opt to sign up for free, inclusive writer's groups that provide informative articles, a chat room, e-mail, and often web-cast events and conferences. Unlike associations and unions, these groups are more casual, and membership is often free. Most of these groups are genre-specific, tailoring to the needs of that community (there are more horror writers than you think).

Joining the American Society of Journalists and Authors (www.asja.org) is not an easy task. You need a minimum of six full-length (1000 words or more) magazine articles from international publications, or two non-fiction books, or non-fiction scripts, or non-fiction Internet magazine articles from major sites (they use Slate and Salon as examples), or a combination of all. Your work is then sent to three members of a committee for evaluation. Once accepted, the dues are steep. So how are the benefits? Phenomenal. Job leads, secret files, newsletters, special members only chat rooms, and Authors Registry membership (facilitating royalty payments), among others. They are the ones on the frontlines, fighting for writers everywhere, so they're good allies to have as a working writer.

The National Writers Union (www.nwu.org) is the union for freelancers working in the US. Membership is limited to those who have published a book, a play, three articles, five poems, a short story, or an equal amount of newsletter, publicity, technical, commercial, government, or institution copy. However, take comfort in the fact that if you are unpublished, but actively seeking publication for those pieces you've written, you may also join. The union provides grievance officers to assist with any problems you may have regarding payment or breach of contract, an agent database to refer to, contract advice, a job hotline, and health and dental plans. They also issue press passes, collect online royalties for members, and distribute publications dealing with the writing industry. Their home page is filled with links to the latest news articles, keeping their members in the know.

You may join the Authors Guild (www.authorsguild.org) on the basis of being a book writer (having been published by an American publishing company within the past seven years) or a freelance writer (having been published three times by general periodicals within the past 18 months). If you've written for the New York Times, Random House, taken a tax deduction for your writing expenses, or written for textbooks and received credit then you've already reaped the benefits of this fair and just-minded organization. The Guild also offers health insurance, prominently features their members' accomplishments online and in a newsletter, and gather often to vote on issues that matter. They have an amazing database full of vital information pertinent to any writer. This informative tax deduction list (of which this book could be considered a part of) is just a taste of Guild's goodwill (www.authorsguild.org/deductionslist.html).

Membership in the National Writers Association (www.nationalwriters.com) provides assistance in self-publishing, allows you to enter contests, employs workers who will help you decipher contracts, and provides you with various publications. They have discounts with major hotels and car rental dealerships, give online writing courses, and sell health insurance policies. A great organization to have on a resume, its networking and marketing opportunities prove this group is worth its weight in gold.

As mentioned earlier, Suite 101 (www.suite101.com) is the ultimate writer's community. Informative articles assisting in everything from screenwriting structure to finding an agent, links to other groups, associations, and databases, chat forums, e-mail, and the opportunity to write for the site all propel this site to the top of the list. Let the editors at Suite 101 guide you through the wonderful world of freelancing on their painless, neatly organized and easy to use site. And if you find yourself humming, don't be alarmed. It means you're enjoying it.

Regionally Focused Freelance Sites

The following sites are regionally focused, a plus should you care to take your freelance pursuits to the next level and work in new media for a living. They provide information on local jobs and support networks, and because they are community-based, expect to feel nurtured and loved in these net "neighborhoods."

New York City: By far the most preeminent site on the web catering to Silicon Alley nobodys and somebodys is the New York New Media Association (www.nynma.org). Membership is suggested, though not required, to partake in the fun, which includes a detailed job bank for writers, programmers, and designers, lists of local events and conferences taking place in Manhattan, advice for newcomers to the field, and low-cost insurance for freelancers. Those are just the freebies. Membership gets you free subscriptions to various e-related magazines, a copy of and a listing in their membership guide, and discounts all around town. The site is user-friendly and thoroughly constructed, and if you can't find a job here, you're not looking hard enough. This site is tight with some of the biggest names in e-business in New York.

Maine: Maine Writers and Publishers Alliance (www.mainewriters.org) works to promote writing and literature within Maine. Composed of writers, publishers, booksellers, librarians, teachers, and the like, the MWPA holds workshops, meetings, and writer's retreats for their members. They are heavy into promoting Maine authors, and are a non-profit book distributor as well.

Florida: Writers, photographers, editors, and others concerned with keeping the quality of writing about the Floridian outdoors top-notch make up the Florida Outdoor Writers Association (www.fowa.org). They feature a consulting service, which divides their working writers into subject-based categories (Looking for a kayak writer? Look no further.), a forum for real-time chats, and profiles on each of their members. Word on the street is their conferences are a lot of fun.

Missouri: The Heartland Writers Guild (www.heartlandwriters.org) is a site where Midwestern writers can get information on getting published, finding an agent, and various other writing-related topics. No job search here, but the

Guild does publish many informative newsletters available to its members.

Nebraska: The Nebraska Center for Writers (NCW) (http://mockingbird.creighton.edu/NCW), like most every association in the Land of Lincoln, is all about pride. (Have you ever attended a Cornhuskers game?) The site premieres Nebraskan authors, past and present, and lists plenty of links to job searches, agent advice, and writer's resources within the state. Their partnership with Amazon allows them to retail books by Nebraskans (they pick up 10% of the sale). They also feature links to hot tourist attractions and popular bookstores.

Colorado: The Colorado Authors' League (www.coloradoauthors.org), founded in 1932, prides itself on being one of the oldest professional writer's groups in the western US. They list their members on the web, including their e-mail address and genre specialty, for those hiring to skim through. They have job opportunities posted and hold various events in the Colorado area for writers to attend each year. Contact someone on the Board of Directors (you'll find the link on the home page) for membership information.

Minneapolis: Membership at the Loft Literary Center (www.loft.org) gets you significantly reduced rates on tuition to classes, magazines, events, and books. If you're a creative or non-fiction memoir writer living in the Twin Cities area, run, don't walk, to your computer and join. Granted, they have no job listings, but they make up for this loss by holding contests and scholarships for fledgling writers, and having IRS 990 forms available for the public to print out at no charge. The Loft was founded in 1974, and has a main office/resource library with books from Minnesotan writers located near the Metrodome (corner of 11th Avenue South and Washington Avenue South) in Minneapolis.

Dallas: The   Dallas   Poets   Community (www.dallaspoets.org) organizes readings, does a bit of publishing, and hosts performances of nationally known poets. In their free time, they hold workshops (which they strongly encourage members to attend), run poetry contests, and volunteer their readers for other poetry events throughout the area.   In other words, this proactive group encourages writers to leave the safety of their CPU, get out there, and perform. Not a bad idea.

Seattle: The   Seattle   Writers   Association (www.scn.org/arts/swa/) offers unique services to its members, residents of the Western Washington region. They encourage members to start up or participate in critique groups, which allow you to get feedback on your work before you send it out. These groups are either genre or proximity based, allowing you to find a group that meets your needs.   SWA also offers marketing workshops to assist authors in finding a potential sales market for their work, a book-reviewing board that reviews full-length manuscripts, and publicity services for recently published authors.

Southern California: The membership dues may be a bit steep to join   the   Independent   Writers   of   Southern   California (www.iwosc.org), but the benefits are good. You have access to a limited job bank (open only to members), can be published on their member's only site page, and are welcomed to a number of

their events. They have a great links page, with the web
addresses of various helpful organizations.

Starting Your Own Auction Site

It's true that even Yahoo!'s auction listings seem barren when
compared to the likes of eBay. With only a few sites holding the
monopoly of online auctioning, it's difficult for other sites,
particularly niche or specialty sites, to get started. Most go
bankrupt before making it to their first birthday. Should you
choose to throw caution to the wind, you can start your own
auction Web site. After registering your domain name and
acquiring some web space, pick up some auction software.
Auction Broker (www.auctionbroker.com) makes software of the
same name designed to grow with your site. Though a bit on the
pricey side, Auction Broker is right for you if investors and
advertising dollars have a soft spot in your hearts (and your bank
accounts).

PS: Believe it or not, the auction community is comprised of
more than just auction sites. The following resources are
designed to make your job as a seller a whole lot easier.

Honesty (www.honesty.com) is the place to go for free counters
and image hosting. They also provide their members with
counter statistics, listing the time and date each item was "hit"
on, and allow their members to list the item, upload the image,
and place a counter on it all in one step.

The Million Auction March (www.millionauctionmarch.com) advocates auction diversity and diluting the potency of some of the auction bigwigs. The site lists alternatives to the main stream, including niche auctions, and charts how many listings the top three auction sites (eBay, Yahoo!, and Amazon) have daily, adding it to an ongoing graph so interested parties can track the rate of growth (no decline here, folks).

Invenna (www.invenna.com) works with eBay to organize and systemize your auctions. Their downloadable software enables you to create better looking item pages, print shipping invoices for customers, and automate e-mail reminders, to be sent to buyers.

Auction Submit (www.auctionsubmit.com) allows you to submit your one listing to multiple auction sites, a plus if you're a "power seller." Saves time and energy, and best of all, the software is free.

uBid Online (www.ubid.com) is a site that sells overstock from various companies with a low starting price.

The 100 Top Auction Sites (www.100topauctionsites.com) are found here.

Auction Talk (www.auctiontalk.com) is a full-fledged community site, with auction news, live chats, and internet auction stock quotes. They are up-to-date with auction news, and like many sites, offer counters and image hosting.

For about $20, Eppraisals (www.eppraisals.com) will appraise your item, explaining the item's history and its worth. You may then attach your Eppraisal to your auction listing. This feature is great for many older antiques and obscure items. Eppraisals also do Second Opinions, where for $15 they will look up an item you are considering bidding on and tell you whether or not it's worth it. They can refer you to an expert in your area for high-end stuff (estate planning, fancy antiques, etc.), and they list bios on all their experts, so you know who you're dealing with.

Square Trade (www.squaretrade.com) serves as an auction mediator between buyer and seller. Should a dispute arise, either the seller or the buyer can file a case. The two then negotiate on a "Case Page," a chat room that serves as neutral ground. If no agreement is reached, an unbiased mediator steps in. The service is free, unless a mediator steps in, but does not hold in a court of law. Square Trade also offers a seal for sellers to place on their listing, proclaiming the seller is reputable and can be trusted.

Become a Part of
OneHourWiz™

*The Legendary, World Famous Method to
Mastering Anything in an Hour*

- **Publish a Quick Tip on an Upcoming Topic
(50-5,000 words)**

- **Submit an Idea to Write an Entire
OneHourWiz**

- **Post Comments on the Topics Mentioned**

- **Read Expanded Excerpts**

- **Free Excerpts From Upcoming Guides**

- **Links for More Information on a Topic**

www.OneHourWiz.com

Order These Other Great
OneHourWiz™ Guides Today!

OneHourWiz: Making Your First Million
By Jon Pirone, ISBN: 1587621037
OneHourWiz: Making Your First Million presents ways for every individual to make their first million. Three main focal areas are covered including investing, starting your own business, and taking equity as a form of compensation. The guide is a very practical and entertaining look at ways for anyone to make their first million. The guide also includes interviews with some of the most successful business people of our time who explain how they "made their first million."

OneHourWiz: Becoming a Techie
By Mary Pyefinch, ISBN: 1587621045
OneHourWiz: Becoming a Techie is a whirlwind tour of computer technology presented in an easy to understand language and format that both technology novices and experts will find useful and entertaining. Readers will learn about computers, networks, programming, the Internet, telecommunications and wireless. After reading this guide, any individual will have the knowledge and guidance to "talk the talk" of the techies. The guide also includes interviews with leading CTOs from companies such as Motley Fool, Symantec, Verisign, Flooz.com and others who help break down the language of the techies!

OneHourWiz: Personal PR & Making a Name For Yourself
By Colleen Inches, ISBN: 1587621061
Have you ever wished you could sell yourself the way advertisers promote products? Wouldn't you love to say, "Hey world, here I am. I'm the best product in the market!" It's no coincidence the most successful people in business do it everyday, and so can you. Colleen Burns Inches shows you how to use self promotion in any career or aspect of your life. Inches, a former television news producer in New York City, gives you step by step instructions on getting attention, recognition and even media coverage for your ideas and events.

OneHourWiz: Internet Freelancing (Easy to Implement Ways to Making a Little or a Lot of Extra Money on the Internet)
By Rachel Vine, ISBN: 1587620030
OneHourWiz: Internet Freelancing contains the most up to date information on how to use the Internet to make a little, or a lot, of extra money on the Internet. The guide covers every opportunity available on the Internet including getting Paid-to-Surf the web, test new Internet products and services, freelance writing, part time consulting opportunities, affiliate programs, or simply getting paid on a monthly basis by having an extra task bar on your browser. Whether you are looking to make an extra $25 a month or an extra $2,500 a month, this guide will pay for itself many times over within the first month alone.

OneHourWiz: Internet and Technology Careers (After the Shakedown)
By April Griffin, ISBN: 1587620049
Want to take advantage of the perks Internet and technology companies have to offer? This guide will help make sure you know what to look for, ask the right questions, and get the right things put into writing so you have your upside (such as options and bonuses) and downside (guaranteed employment clauses) covered. You've heard the hype. Now learn how to use all the buzzwords with authority. Discover the workplace trends - where the hot jobs can be found, the training you need, and the salary to expect. Read interviews with recruiters from international job placement firm Kforce.com as well as computerjobs.com. Regardless of whether you are already in the Internet and technology industry or are looking to break through, this is the guide for you!

OneHourWiz: Stock Options
By Vivian Wagner, ISBN: 1587621053
Stock options are being granted to record numbers of employees, but many people receiving stock options don't really understand what they are. This guide gives you the information you need to make informed decisions about stock options, including how to value them and your company, the difference between Incentive Stock Options (ISOs) and Nonqualified Stock Options (NQSOs), the tax consequences of exercising your options, as well as information for those who want to get into options trading on their own-in an easy to understand language and format. This OneHourWiz guide also includes interviews with noted experts in the field, lawyers from some of the top law firms in the world, CFOs from companies such as Hoovers, LifeMinders,

Register.com, a sample stock option plan from Intel, and worksheets to help you keep track of your stock options.

OneHourWiz: Landing Your First Job
By Andrew Goldsmith, ISBN: 1587620253

Are you a college senior terrified to graduate? Or a freshman with a lot of foresight? This is the guide you need to make sure your first step into the real world takes you in the right direction (and to start thinking ahead to that second step!). You'll get advice from the director of Career Services at one of the hottest Ivy League schools in the country and advice from such experts as the head of recruiting from PriceWaterhouseCoopers. You'll read the stories of people who just a few years ago were standing exactly where you are, and are now establishing themselves at dotcoms, consulting firms, finance jobs, and even in the publishing, entertainment and theater scenes!

OneHourWiz: Public Speaking
By Sporty King, ISBN: 1587621096

OneHourWiz: Public Speaking can help anyone master the art of public speaking. Whether giving a presentation to a few individuals, presenting to thousands of people, or just wanting to speak more confidently to others, this guide will give you all of the keys to success as a public speaker in an easy to understand format and language. This proprietary process used to become a public speaker employed by Sporty King, a renowned public speaker, is sure to get you speaking confidently in no time.

New Titles Available Every Month!

Visit Your Local Bookseller Today!

Visit www.OneHourWiz.com for a Complete List of Titles

OneHourWiz™

The Legendary, World-Famous Method to Mastering Anything in an Hour

How do I become a OneHourWiz?

OneHourWiz is a proven, unique method of learning that focuses on the fundamental principles of a topic, along with advice from industry experts, to master the most important aspects of anything in an hour. Although not always known by the name OneHourWiz, the principles behind this important method of learning have been practiced for decades by leading executives of the world's largest companies, top government officials, federal intelligence agencies, and some of the world's most renowned professors, teachers and visionaries.

Most people do not realize that when trying to learn a new subject or topic, they spend 80% of their time not focusing on the right principles. If they were to receive instruction from the right teachers, focused on the right principles, they could learn anything in a fraction of the time. However, getting all of these industry leaders, teachers and visionaries together would be virtually impossible. Therefore, our OneHourWiz authors collect the most important pieces of information from these individuals, pour through volumes of research, talk with industry leaders and present the material in a condensed and easy to understand format.

So, how is it possible to master anything in an hour? Each OneHourWiz uses a proprietary method that focuses on several core areas including: The 10 Most Important Principles, The History/Background Information, Focal Points/Technique, Interviews With Industry Visionaries, Quick Tips, Case Studies & Worksheets, Resources for Further Research, and a Key Words Glossary so you can "talk the talk." OneHourWiz guides have become overnight classics that remain with our readers for years and years as timeless guides they can always refer back to. So sit back, relax, and enjoy the following pages on your way to becoming a OneHourWiz!